Dedication

For Arjun, who drives me to be better in ways I
never imagined, and for Mansi, who brings so much
light to my heart and soul.

www.theinnerguides.com
www.thejaijais.com

Published by The Jai Jais Ltd
ISBN 978-1-9163242-2-0

The Jai Jais®

CONNECTED
DISCOVERING YOUR INNER GUIDES
BY SEEMA DESAI

ILLUSTRATED BY JAMES BALLANCE

Contents

About The Author

Dr. Seema Desai is a Certified Professional Coach, speaker, writer, dentist, wife, and mother of two in Austin, Texas. Yoga is her passion, as is combatting learning poverty through her volunteer efforts with Pratham USA. She is also passionate about eco-friendly living and chocolate cake, and she loves empowering others with purpose and joy. Seema's happy places include her yoga mat, a tropical beach, and her office couch with a book and a cozy blanket. Her favorite thing to do is snuggle with her husband and kids.

About The Illustrator

James Ballance is an illustrator from Torbay in Devon, now based in London, UK. He studied Illustration with Animation at UWE in Bristol. He loves being on the ocean and getting lost on the moor.

Foreword

We all want our children to be the best version of themselves. But how can we help that happen? As we navigate this uncharted territory of parenting where we focus on building compassion, self-worth, and resilience in the young, finding ways to identify and foster their connection to their inner powers and intuition are necessary foundational skills.

This book is an excellent resource to help us start meaningful conversations with our little ones that will enhance our insight and understanding of them. Harnessing our inner strengths to navigate life's challenges can feel daunting, but Dr. Seema's approach makes it comprehensible for young children and adults alike.

Families will find this book a real treasure trove of help and inspiration, helping both parents and children connect to our higher selves so we can live a life that is joyful, easeful and filled with faith and connection.

This is a book I wish I'd had growing up and is an essential addition to your child's bookshelf.

Tejal V Patel
Author of Meditation for Kids & Host of Time-In Talks Podcast
Instagram @tejalvpatel
www.tejalvpatel.com

2.

How to Use This Book...

For Kid Readers:

Hi, kids! I'm so excited you decided to read this book, because it will show you powerful ways to help make life easier and more fun.

In the first part, you will learn all about something called your Inner Guides, and how they can help you when things get tough.

The second part will show you techniques you can use to connect with your Inner Guides when you need them to help you figure out life's challenges.

The third part will talk about how to stay connected to your Inner Guides even when things are calm and peaceful, so that they are easier to find when you need them.

I suggest reading this book with a parent or another trusted grown-up so that you can learn about your Inner Guides together. This way, your grown-up will know what you need or what you are doing when you decide to use the techniques I share in the book. Maybe they might start to use them, too!

For Adult Readers:

We all want our children to be happy, healthy, and able to adeptly handle all the challenges life holds with love and kindness for themselves and for others. What if you could provide them with the tools to help them do just this? It would be one of the greatest gifts you could possibly give-one that is a vital life skill set that will serve them well in childhood into and through their adult years.

There is a growing body of research showing that mindfulness increases the ability to concentrate and focus, and improves learning, recall, and problem solving. Besides the academic benefits, mindfulness and meditation also help to regulate stress hormones, sleep, and other important functions such as immunity, digestion, and blood pressure. Connecting to our inner world regularly allows us to shift our consciousness higher, leading to self-discovery about what makes us individually and uniquely happy.

I suggest reading this book with your child when you are both calm and receptive. That way, you can learn about the tools described at the same time, and when your child feels challenged, you will know how to refer to them. Especially at first, and particularly for the still-developing brain, when we are faced with challenges, we may have trouble recalling what to do. This is when you can offer loving support with a gentle reminder to turn to the techniques in the book.

Learning anything new can be challenging, especially if it is a subject with which you are not familiar, so be patient when learning and teaching the tools in this book.

Never force your child to use any of the tools presented here. Mindfulness is a journey that must start from within. As caregivers, we are here to guide, not coerce.

Let go of any expectations you may have with regard to the results you would like to see when your child uses these techniques. Often times, when we expect our children to react or behave a certain way, it leads to discord because those expectations were OURS, and never theirs. The goal is to plant seeds of mindfulness. As parents, we have no control over how and when those seeds sprout. The most magical breakthroughs are the ones that come unexpectedly and from within.

If you are worried about using this book because you have never meditated before, relax. Though the techniques described here are presented in a format for children, they can be used by those of any age. I use these techniques on myself and with my children on a regular basis, and have taught other adults to do so as well. If you have a body and are breathing, YOU CAN DO THIS! All it takes is consistency, patience, and trusting the process of self-discovery.

Thank you to children and adults alike for reading this book. I sincerely hope you enjoy it and find it useful.

Love and light to each of you,

Seema ♡

www.drseemadesai.com
IG: @dr.seemadesai

Let's get
CONNECTED
and discover our Inner Guides!

Life as a kid can be pretty great! There are lots of opportunities to learn and do all sorts of cool and interesting things.

It can also be really hard. Sometimes, other kids can be hurtful and make fun of you. Even your best friends can, at times, seem like enemies.

There are times where school seems like a never-ending haze of complicated confusion and pressure. Parents sometimes ask you to do one thing, but mean something else-and then they get upset because they think you are not listening.

Sometimes, it is hard to figure out what to do. Sometimes, it feels like no one in the world will be able to understand.

What if there was a way to help? Let me explain...

I help you discover the world around and within you. If you peel back through the messy layers of your thoughts, you will find space. This space is where you find your Inner Guides. They are an infinite source of wisdom that everyone has- even you!

You can always sense your Guides, though it can be difficult, especially if you are having an encounter with your Inner Guards.

Everyone has Guards and envisions them in different ways. They are a completely normal part of life. They might seem scary at times, but they mean well. When they think you may be threatened, they bring feelings of fear, judgement, guilt, blame, shame, anger, jealousy, and other unpleasant emotions.

Understanding your Guards is an important part of understanding who you are.

Guards can behave much like a puppy that quickly reacts when the doorbell rings, barking loudly with the intention to protect its home and family. Much like the puppy calms down once it sees that the person at the door is a friend, you can calm your Guards by connecting with your Inner Guides.

The more you discover about your own Guards, you will find that acknowledging and accepting your Guards will lead to understanding them. When this happens, they will not seem so scary and invincible.

At any given moment, you can choose to see things through the eyes of a Guard or a Guide. The more you listen to one, the stronger your connection gets with it, and the other one weakens. With practice, you can strengthen your connection with your Guides so that your Guards are less easily heard.

Guides, much like Guards, can look different depending on the situation or person. This is because we are all on our own journeys with our own perspectives.

Cultures all around the world recognize the Guides in many ways. The Inner Guides can be represented by plants, animals, or divine beings, and are celebrated through rituals and festivities throughout the year.

Your Inner Guides have only one job: to help you be the best version of you. They are not really people; they are more like spirits or energies that you can feel. However, you can only feel them when you connect with them.

Your Inner Guides can lead you to solve a problem in different ways depending on which one is doing the talking, and they can even work as a team. By combining different ways of thinking, they help you find your way past life's obstacles.

Allow me to introduce you to your Inner Guides...

Like our Guards, our Guides are unique to each of us. Because of this, you may discover other Guides that I have not introduced here, especially as you learn to explore within yourself.

Let's begin with me, Curiosity. As you may have suspected, I am actually your main Inner Guide.

I help you to ask questions and see things in new and different ways.

I help you approach life without seeing people and circumstances as either good or bad, and right or wrong. I help you to see things with a more open mind. When you let me help, you can learn a lot about yourself and others around you. By asking yourself how you can approach various situations, you are using me, **Curiosity**, to call upon your other Guides so that they can do their jobs.

Fun is a Guide that is really helpful when faced with a task you do not want to do, like taking out the garbage or practicing the piano...

What is something you do not enjoy doing? In what way can you bring fun to that task so that it is more interesting?

Creativity guides you to opportunities that others cannot find. It allows you to discover things that are impossible to see when conforming to the usual or typical ways of thinking and doing.

> Think of a time when you saw
> a solution that others did not.
> What allowed you to do that?
> How can you use that experience
> and apply it to another situation
> in the future?

Balance is important at guiding everything that is going on inside you and in the world around you. It does this by making sure that there is never too much of one thing that may cause you to lose perspective or direction.

Sometimes, inspiration comes from looking to others as examples. How would someone you look up to balance all that is going on well? What are things that make them successful? Which of those things might you be able to use yourself?

Hope helps you to keep going and to trust yourself and the Universe, even when you are unsure of how things will unfold.

Think of a time when things seemed completely out of control. How did it work out? What were some good things that came from it? What can you learn from the good that came from that time that will allow for yourself to have more faith and trust in yourself or others?

Empathy is a very clever and powerful Guide. It travels to places far away and unfamiliar. It is the only Guide that shows you what it is like inside the hearts and minds of other people. Empathy is why you can show loving kindness towards someone you do not actually know, like a lost kitten or the elderly lady that needs help crossing the street. The most amazing aspect of Empathy is that it helps you to understand why others are having or even causing difficulty.

What does showing empathy look like for you? How can feeling and showing empathy help?

Strength is a helpful Guide when you are feeling challenged. Because Strength does not always look like you may think, it can be one of the hardest Guides to find. Strength, in its truest form, is found at the heart of you. It can appear as not only mental or physical strength, but also emotional or spiritual strength. This allows you to calm your Guards with lots of compassion and kindness.

What does being strong mean to you?
What would being strong look and
feel like for you?

Individuality takes you to places within you that are completely unique and is what makes you amazing. Sometimes people might make fun of what is different about you because they may not understand it, but do not let that stop you from exploring what truly makes you special.

What is something you really enjoy about yourself? How does that make you different from others? How can you use that special quality or trait to make the world around you better?

Finding and connecting with your Inner Guides may seem difficult at first, but with practice and consistency, you will start to hear them loud and clear. A good way to start is by sitting in a quiet place. Close your eyes. Sit straight, like there is an invisible thread gently tugging your head toward the sky.

Think about your breath. You can start by paying attention to how it feels to breathe in and out. It is okay if your mind wanders off and thinks about something else. It happens to everyone-kids and adults alike. Just bring your attention back to your breath when you realize that your mind has wandered.

Once you are seated and focused on
your breathing, just ask the question...

You will not hear the answer right away or in the
same way you hear your friends talk to you, but
your Inner Guides will answer.

The answers will come kind of like how you download something; you can only access it when enough information gets sent to your device.

You may be doing something else, like playing a game or eating lunch, when the answer is sent to you - but you will know when you get it.

Being a kid is not always easy, but it can be easier if you let your Inner Guides help!

HOW TO CONNECT WITH YOUR INNER GUIDES WHEN YOUR GUARDS ARE TALKING

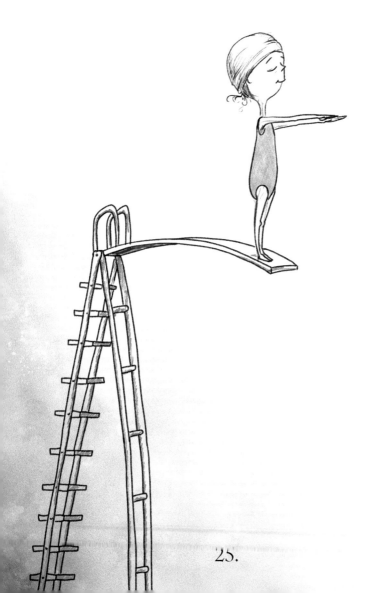

A big part of being human is feeling emotions brought on by Guards. Some of those emotions are unpleasant, and no emotion is wrong or bad. As tempting as it is, if you push your Guards aside, you are actually choosing to ignore what they are saying.

This section of the book is devoted to helping you create awareness of what you are feeling and why, so you do not miss opportunities to listen to the wisdom of your Guides.

Tap Out Your Frustration

Tapping is a great thing to do when you are frustrated because it helps to balance the energy in your body. This allows you to find peace in the present moment so you can hear what your Inner Guides are saying to you.

- Gently tap the middle of your chest with your first two fingers, while bringing attention to how you are breathing and how tapping feels against your chest.

- Tell yourself as you tap, "I'm feeling frustrated, but I know everything will be okay."

- Tap for as long as you need.

Fun Variation: Karate chop your frustration by "chopping" your hands together.

If you don't want to make it obvious that you are tapping, like in the middle of class: Tap your thumb and your fingertips together, one by one by one. Keep going in circles till you feel better.

Feel Your Fear

Fear, anxiety, and worry are common feelings that most people try to push away. However, the more you push those feelings away, the stronger they become. If you give attention to the Guards that cause them, you will calm the feelings themselves. Here's how to do it:

• Find a quiet spot and close your eyes.

• Observe any sensations your body may be feeling, such as sweaty, hot, fast breathing, and so on.

• Try to picture your fear in your body. Where is it? What color is it? How intense or dull is the color?

• Have patience with yourself as you learn to locate and visualize your fear. It is like learning to read, write, or play a new game.

• The more you do it, the easier it gets.

Remember, the goal is to observe, not change, what you are feeling in the present moment.

Now that you have your fear located and visualized, say to it, "Hello Fear, I know you're trying to keep me safe, so it's okay that you're here!" Repeat this as many times as you need.

Bring your attention back to your body. How have your sensations changed?

Feeling your fear (or any unpleasant emotion) takes away the power and control it can have over you. Just like you need to be heard and understood, so does your fear. By accepting and feeling it, you are allowing your Guards to quiet down so that can hear your Inner Guides.

Share Your Guides' Energy

We all have the power to affect each other's moods and energies. Think about a time when your sibling came home from school in a particularly angry mood, or your teacher was not as patient as they normally are. Understandably, situations like this can cause your own Guards to start talking. Here, you have a choice. You can allow your Guards to influence you, or you can help others to feel better by sharing the Inner Guides' energy within you.

Here is how!

• Take a moment to connect with your Inner Guides when others are being influenced by their Guards. This is a powerful way of ensuring that your own Guards stay at rest. You may try the tapping or breathing techniques mentioned earlier. As you gain practice with connecting, you will discover even more connection tools that work well for you.

• Next, envision yourself glowing with a beautiful, golden light. Tell yourself, "I bring peace, I bring love, I bring kindness to those around me, both near and far away."

• See what insights your Inner Guides give you about the other person. Often, simply recognizing and acknowledging that they are upset will help them to feel better and can effectively help their Guards relax. You may even be able to shift them to a place where they can start to connect with their own Inner Guides!

This tool can be a bit tricky. Sometimes, it works like magic, and other times, it will not seem to have worked at all. That does not mean it has not. It can take a few minutes, or even hours, for an act of kindness to sink in. Remember, we can not control how others feel or think, but in any situation, we can choose whether we connect to our Guards or our Guides.

NOTE: Sometimes, simply offering a smile can make a remarkable difference for someone. Try it the next time you encounter a grouchy person at the grocery store or classmate in the hall!

HOW TO STAY CONNECTED
WITH YOUR INNER GUIDES

It is good to be able to stay connected with your Guides throughout the day, so that when challenges do come up, you can handle them with more ease, or maybe even avoid them altogether! The following tools can be used any time to encourage your Guards to keep resting.

Keep A Gratitude Journal

This works if you do it consistently.

Keep a journal by your bedside.

Every day, either before bed or when you wake up, take a minute to close your eyes and think of one thing for which you feel truly grateful.

Now, write it down in your journal. It could be anything as long as it is something for which you are genuinely grateful. Rattling off something that you "should" be grateful for will not really get the job done. This is best done with intention.

Take a moment to **REALLY** think about it.

We have all felt that feeling of gratefulness - that feeling that your heart may just burst because you are so thankful for something.

You can use this tool at any time during the day, but the reasons to write it down specifically before bed or after waking up are these:

Doing it at a specific time of each day helps make it a great habit!

Writing it down actually has more of an effect on your brain.

Doing it upon waking helps set your intentions and goals for the day, and gets you off to a good start.

Writing it down before bed changes your mindset before you turn off for the night, and helps you sleep better, meaning you are better-equipped to handle the next day.

Why?

Because thinking about what you are grateful for changes the way your mind sees things.

If you are always encouraging your mind to see the good, there is a lot less time to focus on what you do not have or what is wrong.

Practicing gratitude regularly changes how your mind sees things. If you are constantly encouraging your mind to focus on the good, there is less time for your Guards to pipe up with what things are not.

When you are in "grateful mode", you will be able to be connected to what your Inner Guides are telling you.

38.

Check into Your Body

While listening to your body is great to do when you are feeling stress or fear, listening to it all the time helps you avoid problems altogether by allowing you to foresee potential challenges.

Think of a time when you were hungry, but too busy to realize it. Was it harder to listen in class or be kind on the playground? Maybe you wound up fighting with Mom or Dad.

There are probably many times where this has happened, and eating something would have made all the difference.

If you start to check into your body at the same time every day, you may start to notice things like, "Hey, I'm getting kind of hungry!" or "Some water would be nice!" You may even start to notice certain patterns and learn more about what your body needs.

Tap the Replay Button

We all have experienced times where embarrassment or anger made us say and do things we normally would not. Think about a time when things went so badly that you wish you could just go back and do them differently... like saying your brother is the worst brother in the world, or telling your best friend that you do not want to be friends anymore.

41.

While you cannot go back in time and actually redo things, you can replay them and imagine a different ending in your mind. If you are not sure how you would have liked the story to end, you can ask your Inner Guides for help. By thinking about a time that was particularly difficult for you, and allowing your mind to see a different ending, you are strengthening your connection to your Guides. Envisioning a new ending will allow your brain to respond in a more favorable way the next time a similar situation arises.

Put on Your Perspective Goggles

Have you ever noticed that when you sit in a different spot than you normally do on the couch or at school, things seem really different? What about when you come home from the opposite direction from which you usually come?

You may notice some new or interesting things about your surroundings.

If you put on your Perspective Goggles and try to see things from another person's point of view, you will find that you understand why they say or do the things that they do. It will be much easier to see these situations as opportunities to learn and find creative outcomes.

Putting on your Perspective Goggles is great to do any time, especially when you feel your Guards are about to start talking. However, it is a tool best learned when calm, or perhaps in conjunction with the "Tap the Replay Button" exercise, so you can hear your Inner Guides as they show you what others may have been thinking or feeling.

Ask yourself why your mom seems frustrated when calling you for dinner. She might be feeling unheard because no one responded the first few times she called for everyone!

Remembering to celebrate your efforts each time you try and connect with your Inner Guides is much like remembering to save your work on the computer. Each moment of awareness builds on the ones of the past, just like each letter builds on the words you are typing.

Connecting with your Inner Guides takes practice and patience. Sometimes, you will be able to hear them well, and at others, you will not. This happens to adults, too, and is totally normal.

The key is to keep practicing, because your Inner Guides are always there for you!

You can always refer back to this book to help you remember how to connect to your Inner Guides. After some practice, you will be able to teach your family, teachers, and friends how to do this, too!

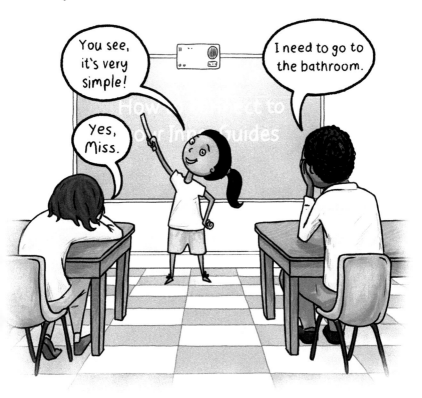

Each of us has a very special gift to share. Practicing these tools will help you use your special gifts to make the world better and brighter in your own unique way!

Acknowledgements

First and foremost, I'd like to thank my parents, parents-in-law, husband, children, and very large extended family for loving me unconditionally, and for shaping me into the person that I am today. It is because of you that I am inspired to help others elevate their consciousness and discover their own inner peace, both with this book and in all my other endeavors.

I would also like to thank my life coach, Jonathan Troen. Many of his techniques and teachings were inspirational for the exercises presented in this book. He has taught me so much about just how important it is to live life with love and kindness- not just for others, but for yourself, as well.

This book would never have come to life had it not been for Sunita Shah and James Ballance. They saw something in me that I never would have, and I'm so grateful to them for the opportunity that they gave me to write this book.

Additionally, I'd like to thank my dear friend Tejal V. Patel, not only for agreeing to write the foreword for this book, but for always teaching me in the most amazing ways about all things spiritual.

And of course, I would like to thank you, the reader. Without you, this book is simply words on a page. Because of you, this book has meaning and significance. I truly hope it changes the way you see life, that it inspires you to realize just how much greatness is inside of you, and that it empowers you to help others realize the same greatness in themselves.

Namaste!